SKY WATCHING

The Sun

Carmel Reilly

CHILDREN'S LIBRARY

Marshall Cavendish
Benchmark
New York

This edition first published in 2012 in the United States of America by
Marshall Cavendish Benchmark
An imprint of Marshall Cavendish Corporation

Website: www.marshallcavendish.us

This publication represents the opinions and views of the author based on Carmel Reilly's personal experience, knowledge, and research. The information in this book serves as a general guide only. The author and publisher have used their best efforts in preparing this book and disclaim liability rising directly and indirectly from the use and application of this book.

Other Marshall Cavendish Offices: Marshall Cavendish International (Asia) Private Limited, 1 New Industrial Road, Singapore 536196 • Marshall Cavendish International (Thailand) Co Ltd. 253 Asoke, 12th Flr, Sukhumvit 21 Road, Klongtoey Nua, Wattana, Bangkok 10110, Thailand • Marshall Cavendish (Malaysia) Sdn Bhd, Times Subang, Lot 46, Subang Hi-Tech Industrial Park, Batu Tiga, 40000 Shah Alam, Selangor Darul Ehsan, Malaysia

Marshall Cavendish is a trademark of Times Publishing Limited

All websites were available and accurate when this book was sent to press.

Library of Congress Cataloging-in-Publication Data

Reilly, Carmel, 1957-
  The sun / Carmel Reilly.
     p. cm. — (Sky watching)
  Includes index.
  Summary: "Provides scientific information about the sun"—Provided by publisher.
  ISBN 978-1-60870-584-9
  1. Sun—Juvenile literature. 2. Astronomy—Observers' manuals—Juvenile literature. I. Title.
  QB521.5.R45 2012
  523.7—dc22
                              2010044019

Publisher: Carmel Heron
Commissioning Editor: Niki Horin
Managing Editor: Vanessa Lanaway
Project Editor: Tim Clarke
Editor: Paige Amor
Proofreader: Helena Newton
Designer: Polar Design
Page layout: Romy Pearse
Photo Researcher: Legendimages
Illustrator: Adrian Hogan
Production Controller: Vanessa Johnson

Printed in China

Acknowledgments
The author and publisher are grateful to the following for permission to reproduce copyright material:

Front cover photograph: The sun setting over the ocean © Shutterstock/Serg64.

Photographs courtesy of: Dreamstime/Mturner629, **27**, /Solarwindstudios, **25**; iStockphoto/Kirill Putchenko, **11**, **14**, /Mike Sonnenberg, **5** (bottom), /Sergii Tsololo, border element throughout, /Zuki, **16**; NASA/ESA/SOHO, **18**, /JAXA , **19**, /Lunar and Planetary Laboratory, **5** (top); Photolibrary/DV, **15**, /Fotosearch, **17**, /RKN, **10**, /Science Photo Library/Eckhard Slawik, **9**; Shutterstock/Liudmila Gridina, **8**, /Viktar Malyshchyts, **29**, /OlesiaRu&IvanRu, **5** (top inset), /Serg64, **1**.

Please Note
At the time of printing, the Internet addresses appearing in this book were correct. Owing to the dynamic nature of the Internet, however, we cannot guarantee that all these addresses will remain correct.

CONTENTS

Glossary Words
Words that are printed in **bold** are explained in the glossary on page 31.

What Does It Mean?
Words that are within a **box** are explained in the "What Does It Mean?" panel at the bottom of the page.

SKY WATCHING

When we sky watch, we look at everything above Earth. This includes what is in Earth's **atmosphere** and the objects we can see beyond it, in space .

Why Do We Sky Watch?

Sky watching helps us to understand more about Earth's place in space. Earth is our home. It is also a planet that is part of a space neighborhood called the **solar system**. When we sky watch we learn about Earth, and our neighbors inside and outside the solar system.

What Objects Are in the Sky?

There are thousands of objects in the sky above Earth. These are Earth's neighbors—the Sun, the Moon, planets, stars, and flying space rocks (**comets**, **asteroids**, and **meteoroids**). Some can be seen at night and others can be seen during the day. Although some are visible with the human eye, all objects must be viewed through a telescope to be seen more clearly.

When and How Can We See Objects in the Sky?

Object in the Sky	Visible with Only the Human Eye 👁	Visible Only through a Telescope 🔭	Visible during the Day ☀	Visible at Night 🌙
Earth's Atmosphere	✗	✗	✗	✗
Sun	✓ (Do not view directly)	✗ (View only with a special telescope)	✓	✗
Moon	✓	✗	Sometimes	✓
Planets	Sometimes	Sometimes	Sometimes	✓
Stars	Sometimes	Sometimes	✗	✓
Comets	Sometimes	Sometimes	✗	✓
Asteroids	Sometimes	Sometimes	✗	✓
Meteoroids	Sometimes	Sometimes	✗	✓

WHAT DOES IT MEAN?

space The area in which the solar system, stars, and galaxies exist, also known as the universe.

THE SUN

The Sun is a space object that can be seen in the sky without a telescope. It is only visible during the day.

Sun Watching

People have always watched the Sun. However, it was only when telescopes were invented 500 years ago that astronomers were finally able to see just a little of its surface. The Sun is very dangerous to look at directly, which made it hard to study. Now, thanks to space exploration and telescopes that allow people to view the Sun's surface safely, they have been able to find out much more about our local star. Today people know what the Sun is made of, what its atmosphere is like, and how it affects Earth.

Sky watching can be done during the day or night, with or without a telescope. Just look up!

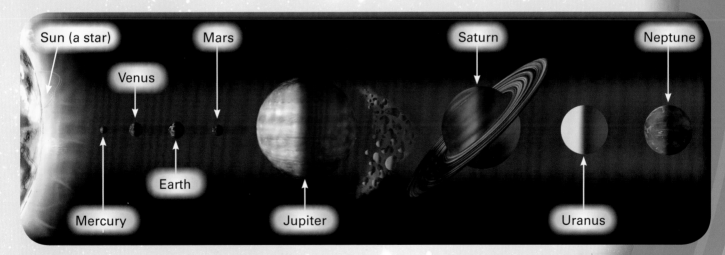

Sun (a star)   Venus   Mars   Saturn   Neptune

Mercury   Earth   Jupiter   Uranus

The Sun is 750 times bigger than everything else in the solar system put together. This diagram shows the approximate relative sizes of the Sun and the planets. The distances between them are not to scale.

WHAT IS THE SUN?

The Sun is the star at the center of our solar system. It is a huge ball of hot **gases** that gives off energy. The Sun was formed 4.7 billion years ago.

The Sun Is a Star

The Sun is one of billions of stars in our galaxy. Stars like the Sun begin life as a cloud of gases and dust, called a **nebula**. The nebula is then pulled together by gravity. Over time, it forms a hot ball of gas, called a **protostar**. Over millions and even billions of years, this protostar slowly forms into a star.

Stars appear as tiny dots of light in the night sky. Because we are so close to our star, the Sun, we see it as a large, glowing ball in the daytime sky. The Sun is the source of all Earth's energy.

4. A huge ball of hot gases, called a protostar, forms at its center. Cooler dust and gases spin around the outside.

3. The nebula begins to spin and grow very hot.

5. The dust and gases flatten into a spinning disc.

2. The pull of gravity begins to shrink the nebula and brings it together.

1. The Sun begins life as a swirling nebula.

6. The ball of hot gases in the center becomes our Sun. Planets and other space objects form from the dust that spins around it.

 It took billions of years for our Sun to form.

WHAT DOES IT MEAN ?

galaxy A large system of space objects, including stars, planets, gas, and dust.

gravity The force that attracts all objects toward each other.

The Sun Is at the Center of Our Solar System

A solar system is made up of a star that has planets in **orbit** around it. Earth is one of eight planets and hundreds of other space objects that orbit our star, the Sun. These objects orbit the Sun because its gravity pulls on them as they move through space. The Sun's **gravitational pull** keeps them on the same orbital paths and stops them from flying off into space.

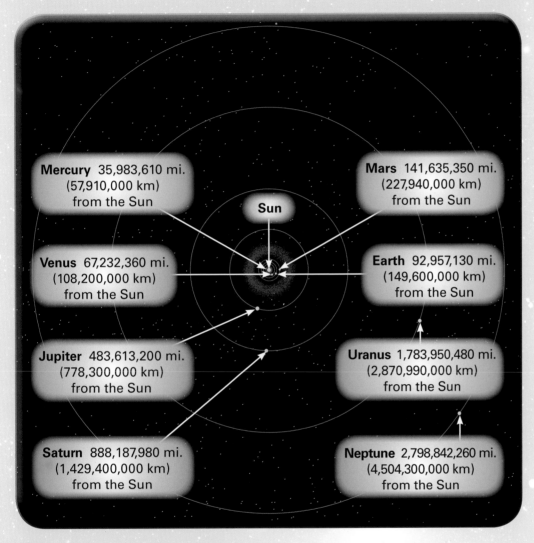

Mercury 35,983,610 mi.
(57,910,000 km)
from the Sun

Venus 67,232,360 mi.
(108,200,000 km)
from the Sun

Jupiter 483,613,200 mi.
(778,300,000 km)
from the Sun

Saturn 888,187,980 mi.
(1,429,400,000 km)
from the Sun

Sun

Mars 141,635,350 mi.
(227,940,000 km)
from the Sun

Earth 92,957,130 mi.
(149,600,000 km)
from the Sun

Uranus 1,783,950,480 mi.
(2,870,990,000 km)
from the Sun

Neptune 2,798,842,260 mi.
(4,504,300,000 km)
from the Sun

 This illustration gives the distance of each planet from the Sun in miles (mi.) and kilometers (km).

The Sun Is a Ball of Hot Gases

Like all stars, the Sun is a ball of hot gases. Gravity pulls these gases together, creating a type of energy that we call nuclear energy. This energy leaves the Sun in the form of heat and light. It is the light and warmth of the Sun that we can feel on Earth and that provides us with energy.

 **WHAT DOES IT MEAN**

nuclear energy Energy in the form of heat that is produced when two or more atoms (the smallest part of substance) join together to form a single new atom.

WHAT DOES THE SUN LOOK LIKE FROM EARTH?

The Sun is the largest and brightest space object in our daytime sky. We see it as a large, glowing ball. Sometimes the Sun is blocked by clouds or bad weather, making it difficult to view. It can also be blocked by the Moon, which causes a solar eclipse.

The Sun Seems to Change Color and Size

From Earth, the Sun can look white, yellow, or even orange or red at sunset. This is because of the way the Sun's light reflects through Earth's atmosphere. The color and size of the Sun seems to change depending on the distance light rays have to travel through the atmosphere.

Sun Fact

On average, the Sun is 93,205,680 mi. (150,000,000 km) from Earth. It would take more than 160 years to drive there in a car.

The surface of the Sun was first seen through a telescope in 1613.

The Sun Can Be Blocked by Clouds

Sometimes the Sun is blocked from view by clouds. Even on sunny days, clouds often pass across the face of the Sun. On very cloudy days, the Sun may not appear at all. During storms, the sky can become very dark because the clouds are so thick that they let very little sunlight through.

The Sun Can Be Blocked by the Moon

When the Moon passes between the Sun and Earth, a solar eclipse occurs. During a solar eclipse, the Moon's shadow falls across the Earth. When the Sun is completely covered, the sky becomes dark and stars can be seen. The darkness can last for around seven minutes. There are about four or five solar eclipses a year.

The first recorded solar eclipse occurred more than 4,000 years ago. It was recorded by Chinese astronomers. For about 3,000 years, astronomers have recorded information about previous eclipses and the movements of Earth and the Moon. They do this to predict when future solar eclipses will occur.

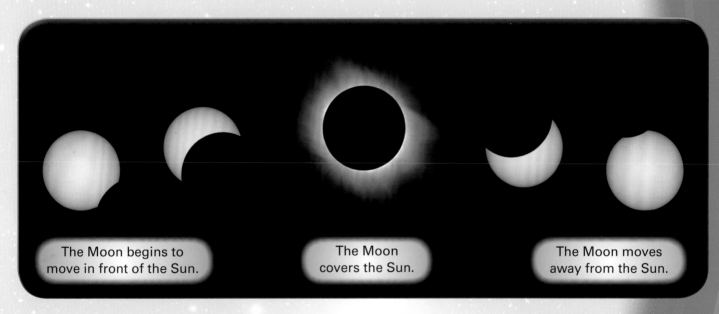

The Moon begins to move in front of the Sun.

The Moon covers the Sun.

The Moon moves away from the Sun.

It takes about an hour for the Moon to cross the face of the Sun.

FAMOUS SKY WATCHERS

In 1543 Nicolaus Copernicus, a Polish astronomer, put forth the idea that Earth and the other known planets orbited around the Sun. Until then, people believed the Sun and planets orbited around Earth.

WHAT IS THE SUN MADE OF?

From Earth, we cannot tell what is inside the Sun. Scientists have found out about the Sun by using telescopes and with information gathered from space exploration. They believe that the Sun is made up of three layers of gas. These are the core, the radiative zone, and the convective zone. The surface of the Sun is known as the photosphere.

The Sun Has a Core

The center of the Sun is called the core. The core makes up only one quarter of the Sun. However, because it is full of thick, tightly packed gases, it is very heavy. It makes up more than half of the Sun's weight.

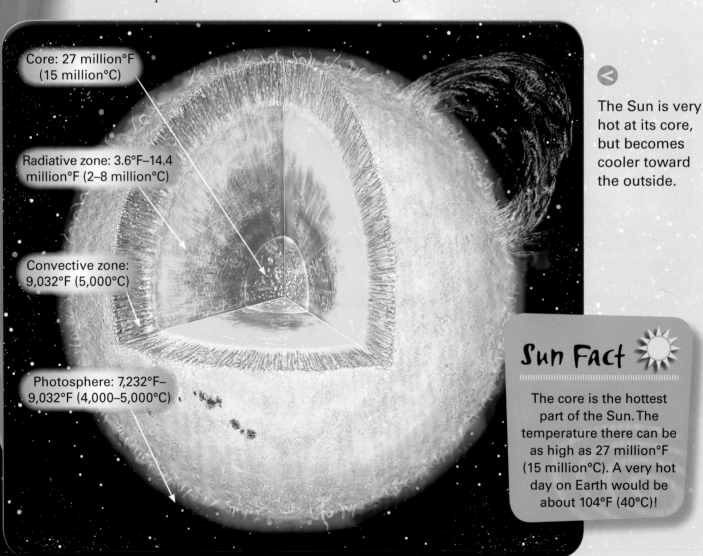

Core: 27 million°F (15 million°C)

Radiative zone: 3.6°F–14.4 million°F (2–8 million°C)

Convective zone: 9,032°F (5,000°C)

Photosphere: 7,232°F–9,032°F (4,000–5,000°C)

The Sun is very hot at its core, but becomes cooler toward the outside.

Sun Fact

The core is the hottest part of the Sun. The temperature there can be as high as 27 million°F (15 million°C). A very hot day on Earth would be about 104°F (40°C)!

The Sun's Energy Comes from the Core

The Sun's energy is made in its core. At the core, gravity pulls all of the gases tightly together, causing incredible pressure and heat. This starts a process in which some gases in the Sun change and release nuclear energy.

FAMOUS SKY WATCHERS

It was only in 1904 that Ernest Rutherford, a British–New Zealand scientist, suggested that the Sun's energy might come from **radiation** it produced in its core.

V Every second of each day the Sun pumps out enough energy to supply Earth with 1,000 years of power.

The Sun Has a Radiative Zone

The Sun's radiative zone lies just outside the core. It makes up about one third of the area inside the Sun. The energy produced in the core travels outward, through the radiative zone. It is called the radiative zone because energy here takes the form of radiation. This means that it travels as rays or waves. Energy moves slowly here because it keeps smashing into the radiative zone's dense gases.

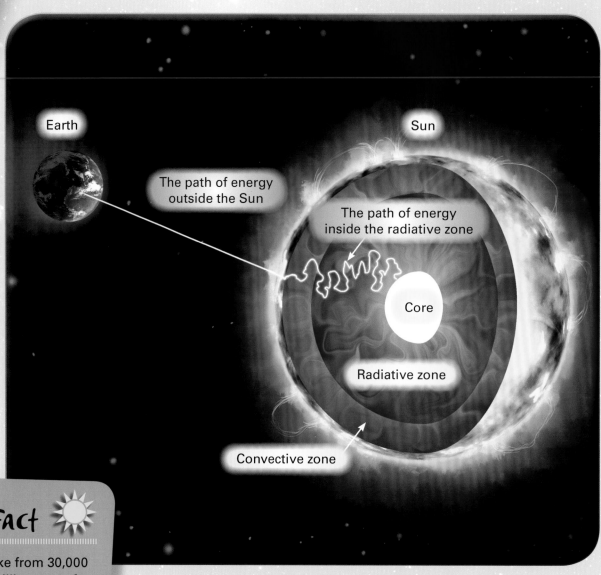

Earth

Sun

The path of energy outside the Sun

The path of energy inside the radiative zone

Core

Radiative zone

Convective zone

Radiation slowly loses energy as it makes its way through the radiative zone.

The Sun Has a Convective Zone

The Sun's convective zone lies just below its surface. It makes up more than half of the area inside the Sun. In the convective zone, the energy is carried along on rising and falling currents of **plasma**, which makes the Sun's surface look like it is boiling.

Energy in the convective zone moves faster than in the radiative zone. This is because it follows a more direct path. It only takes about a week for the energy to travel through the convective zone to the photosphere.

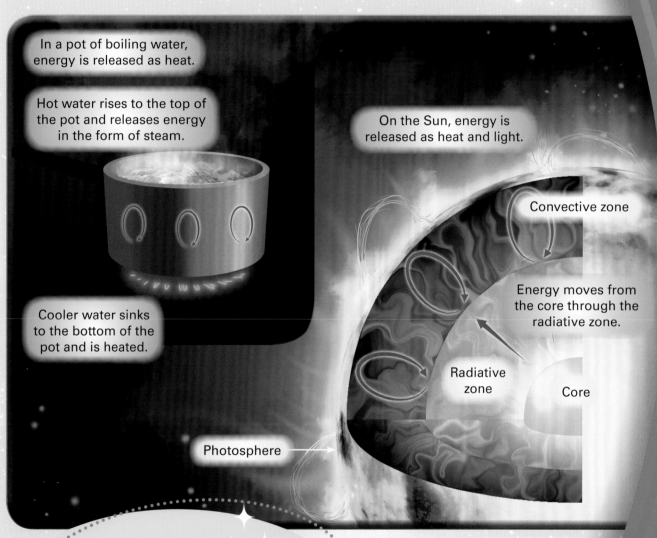

In a pot of boiling water, energy is released as heat.

Hot water rises to the top of the pot and releases energy in the form of steam.

Cooler water sinks to the bottom of the pot and is heated.

On the Sun, energy is released as heat and light.

Convective zone

Energy moves from the core through the radiative zone.

Radiative zone

Core

Photosphere

The way energy travels in the Sun's convective zone is like the movement of boiling water in a pot.

FAMOUS SKY WATCHERS

National Aeronautics and Space Administration (NASA) scientists study the Sun. Although they cannot see inside it, they are able to take measurements of vibrations on the Sun's surface to build a picture of what it is like inside the Sun.

WHAT IS THE SURFACE OF THE SUN LIKE?

From Earth, the Sun is seen as a shining ball of light. Viewed through a space telescope with a special filter, the surface has a bubbly, orangey-yellow appearance, with dark patches that come and go.

The Surface of the Sun Is a Sea of Gas

The Sun's surface is known as the photosphere. Because the Sun is not a solid object, the photosphere is not a hard surface. It is a 311-mile (500-km) thick layer of gases that lies between the top of the convective zone and the Sun's atmosphere. The photosphere has a surface temperature of about 11,732°F (5,500°C).

The Surface of the Sun Is a Shining Ball of Light

The photosphere is transparent, or see-through. It allows the energy inside the Sun to escape out into space in the form of heat and light. The reason we see the Sun's surface as a bubbly orange-yellow is because we are seeing the energy activity from the convective layer below the photosphere.

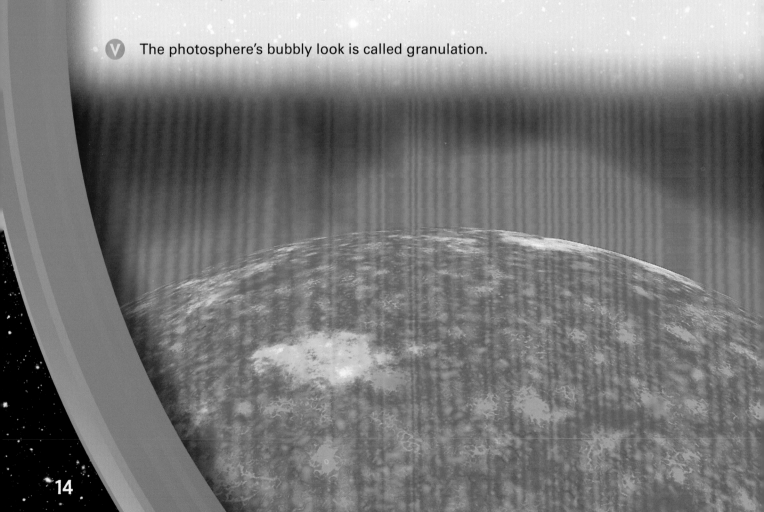

V   The photosphere's bubbly look is called granulation.

14

The Surface of the Sun Has Sunspots

Sunspots are temporary dark patches that can be seen from time to time on the surface of the Sun. They are caused by the Sun's **magnetic fields**. These fields stop the heat inside the Sun from getting to the surface by pulling plasma back toward them. Because areas affected by magnetic fields are cooler than the rest of the photosphere, they look darker.

Sunspots range from less than 621 mi. (1,000 km) wide to groups of joined sunspots that are 62,137 mi. (100,000 km) wide. Sunspots grow smaller and bigger as they move across the photosphere. They can last from a few hours to weeks at a time.

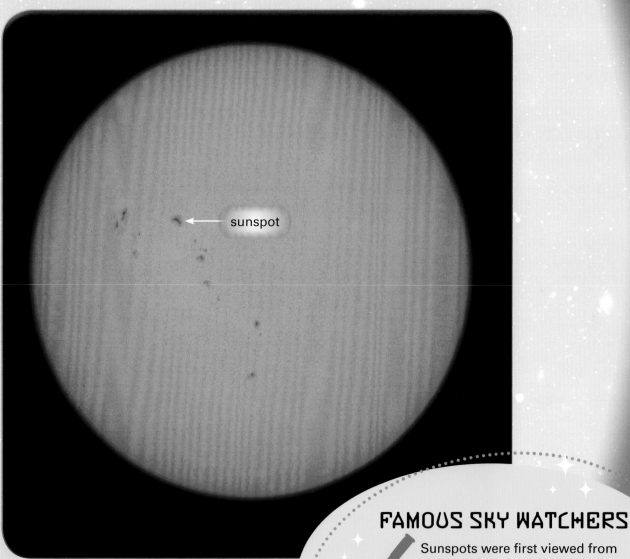

← sunspot

⋀ Sunspots are about 2,732°F (1,500°C) cooler than the areas around them.

FAMOUS SKY WATCHERS

Sunspots were first viewed from Earth in 1513 by the Italian astronomer Galileo Galilei. He observed the sunspots and made drawings of them using a telescope that he built to view the Sun.

WHAT ARE CONDITIONS LIKE NEAR THE SUN?

The Sun's atmosphere is thinner, hotter, and more explosive than Earth's. It cannot support life. The Sun's atmosphere is made up of the chromosphere and the corona, which stretch far out into space. A great deal of activity takes place at both levels of the atmosphere.

The Sun Is Surrounded by a Chromosphere

The chromosphere is a thin mixture of gases. It starts above the photosphere and stretches about 3,107 mi. (5,000 km) into space. Its temperature ranges from about 7,232°F (4,000°C) near the surface, to about 900,032°F (500,000°C) as it reaches the corona.

Astronomers using powerful telescopes are able to see jets and loops of gas, or plasma, that rise up from the chromosphere into the corona.

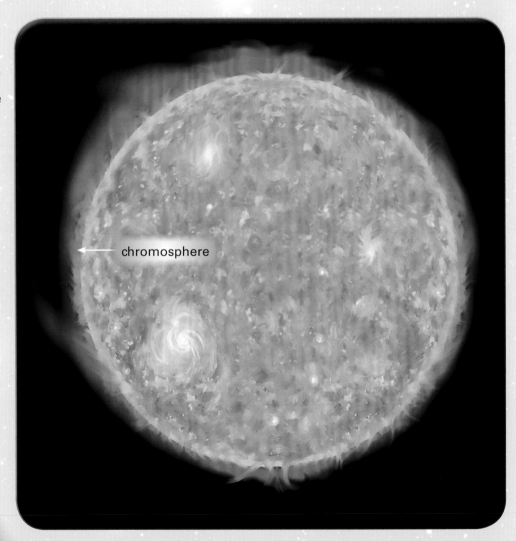

The chromosphere is an orange-red colored irregular layer of gas.

chromosphere

The Sun Is Surrounded by a Corona

The corona is the outer layer of the Sun's atmosphere. It starts above the chromosphere and stretches millions of miles into space. The corona has far less plasma than the rest of the atmosphere. It is also very hot, with temperatures that can reach up to 3.6 million°F (2 million°C). Its outer edges are constantly being blown away by the solar wind.

▼ During a solar eclipse, when the Moon passes between Earth and the Sun, it is possible to see the Sun's corona without using a telescope.

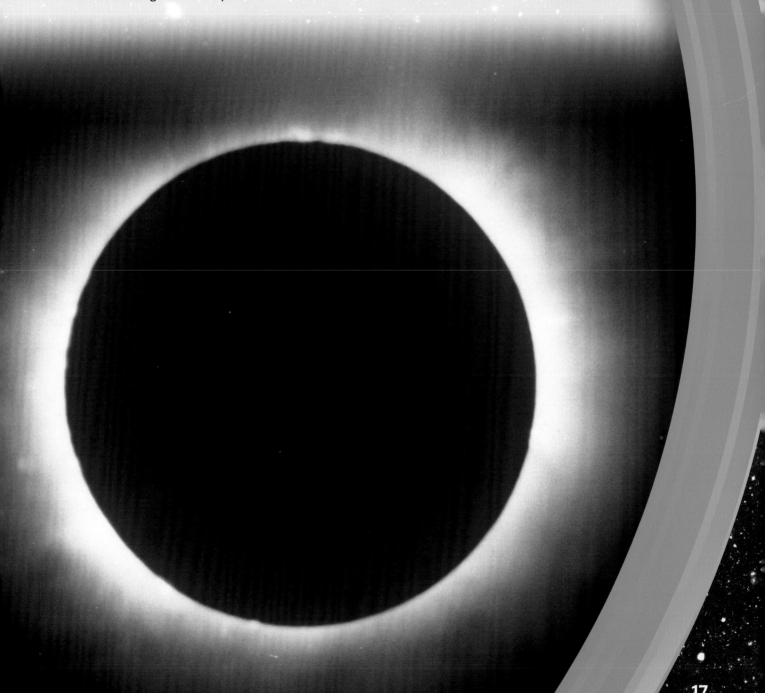

There Is Activity in the Sun's Atmosphere

Activity in the Sun's atmosphere includes prominences, coronal mass ejections, spicules that shoot into the air, and solar flares and solar wind that can even affect Earth.

Prominences Shoot from the Chromosphere

Prominences are huge waves of gas that shoot up from the chromosphere and float in the corona. They stretch for many thousands of miles (kilometers) and can last for many weeks. They are formed by magnetic fields over sunspots.

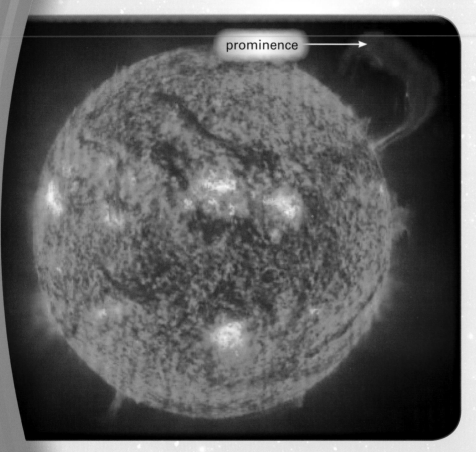

prominence

Sun Fact

Some scientists believe that the activity in the Sun's atmosphere can affect weather on Earth. When there is less activity on the Sun, Earth's temperature seems to be cooler.

Prominences can take the shape of huge loops or arches.

Coronal Mass Ejections Bubble Up from the Surface

Coronal mass ejections are huge bubbles of gas. They rise up from the Sun's surface and travel through the corona and into space.

Spicules

Spicules are tall spikes of gas that shoot from the chromosphere into the corona. Each spicule lasts for about 15 minutes.

Solar Flares Explode in the Chromosphere

Solar flares are explosions that take place in the chromosphere, above where sunspots form. They appear like a flash of light and can last for ten minutes or more.

Solar Wind Blows into Space

Solar wind blows into space from the corona. Solar wind is not like wind on Earth because it is made up of **magnetic currents** and **electric currents**. Solar wind can travel as far as 9 billion mi. (15 billion km) from the Sun. Earth's atmosphere shields us from most of its effects.

V Large solar flares can send out enough magnetic energy and radiation to reach Earth and affect radio communications. This image shows a number of solar flares on the Sun.

FAMOUS SKY WATCHERS

Between 1959 and 1968 NASA sent a series of pioneer space probes to measure the solar wind and magnetic fields.

HOW DOES THE SUN MOVE?

Scientists have discovered that, like Earth, the Sun **rotates**. It also moves through space, orbiting the Milky Way.

The Sun Rotates

It takes about one month for the Sun to fully rotate. Because it is made of gas, some parts of it rotate more quickly than others. Gas near the Sun's [**equator**] takes about twenty-five days to rotate. Gas at the top and bottom of the Sun takes thirty-five days to completely rotate.

V   By studying the surface of the Sun, scientists discovered that different parts of the Sun rotate at different speeds.

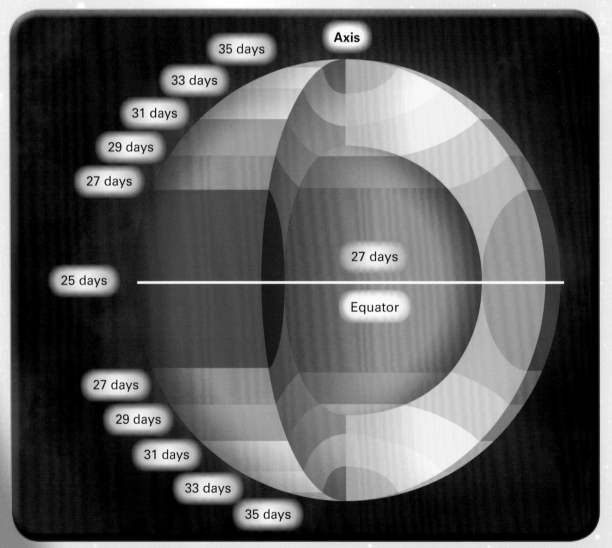

Axis

35 days
33 days
31 days
29 days
27 days

25 days

27 days

Equator

27 days
29 days
31 days
33 days
35 days

WHAT DOES IT MEAN ?   [**equator**]   An imaginary line around the middle or widest part of a round space object, such as a star or planet.

The Sun Orbits the Milky Way

The Sun and all of our solar system is part of a rotating, disc-shaped galaxy called the Milky Way. As the Sun moves through space, it orbits the center of the Milky Way. The gravitational pull of the Milky Way keeps the Sun on the same orbital path and stops it from flying off into space.

V The Sun lies on the Orion Arm of the Milky Way, about halfway from the galaxy's center.

Sun Fact

The Sun moves through space at 150 mi. (240 km) a second. At this speed it takes about 220 million years for the Sun to orbit the Milky Way.

The arms are made up of stars, gas, and dust.

Central galactic bulge (galaxy's center)

Sagittarius Arm

Orion Arm

Our Sun

Perseus Arm

HOW DOES THE SUN AFFECT EARTH?

The Sun affects Earth in many ways. As the center of our solar system, the Sun keeps Earth stable in its orbit and provides us with energy. In turn, Earth's atmosphere works with the Sun to make the right conditions for life.

The Sun's gravity helps Earth maintain its orbit.

The Sun is used to mark days and years on Earth.

The Sun creates seasons on Earth.

The Sun gives Earth energy.

The Sun works with Earth's atmosphere to create weather and stable temperatures.

The Sun is important to Earth in many ways.

The Sun Helps Earth Maintain Its Orbit

The Sun's gravitational pull keeps Earth on the same orbital path and stops it from drifting off into space. Earth's orbit helps to keep it stable and create regular conditions, such as day and night, and the seasons.

What If There Were No Sun?

Without the Sun, Earth would not keep its orbit and it would drift off into space. Days, nights, and seasons would not occur regularly because Earth would not be spinning or orbiting the Sun. Earth would also be in more danger of colliding with other space objects.

The Sun Gives Earth Energy

All energy on Earth comes from the Sun. Plants get their energy directly from the Sun, while animals and people get their energy from plants and other animals. Animals and people also need direct sunlight to help them process the vitamins and minerals that their bodies need.

What If There Were No Sun?

Without the Sun, Earth would not have the energy it needs to support life. Plants would die, and the animals and people who rely on those plants to live would also die.

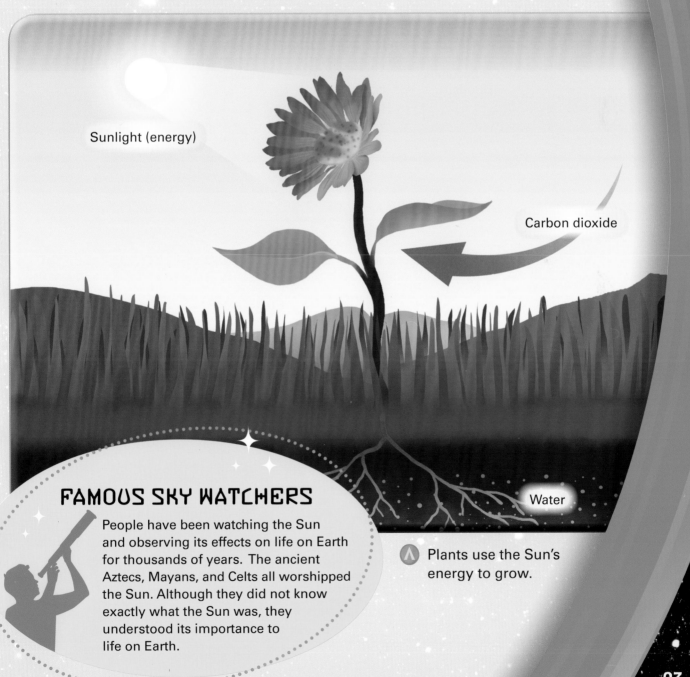

Sunlight (energy)

Carbon dioxide

Water

Plants use the Sun's energy to grow.

FAMOUS SKY WATCHERS

People have been watching the Sun and observing its effects on life on Earth for thousands of years. The ancient Aztecs, Mayans, and Celts all worshipped the Sun. Although they did not know exactly what the Sun was, they understood its importance to life on Earth.

The Sun Works with Earth's Atmosphere

The Sun and Earth's atmosphere work together to create daylight, weather, and stable temperatures. Together they also give us blue skies, sunsets, and colorful auroras, or light shows.

The Sun Creates Weather on Earth

The Sun heats Earth, but not all parts at the same time. When one part is warm, another part is cold. This creates air movement, which keeps temperatures even. When the Sun heats water on Earth, it rises into the air and becomes clouds. This water then falls again as rain or snow.

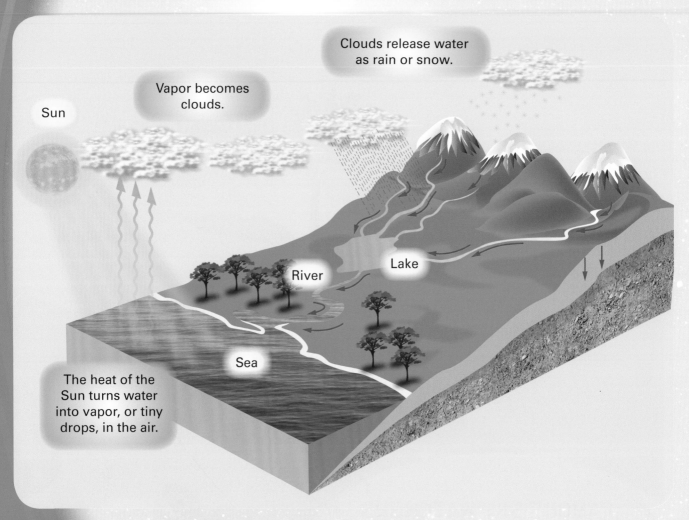

Clouds release water as rain or snow.

Vapor becomes clouds.

Sun

Lake

River

Sea

The heat of the Sun turns water into vapor, or tiny drops, in the air.

The Sun plays an important part in the water cycle on Earth.

The Sun Gives Us Blue Skies and Sunsets

In space the sky looks black, but on Earth the sky appears blue. This is because some of the colors that make up the Sun's light are scattered, and reflected around in our atmosphere.

The Sun Creates Auroras

Auroras are colored lights that can be seen in the sky near the Arctic and Antarctic. They are caused when magnetic **particles** from the solar wind are trapped in Earth's atmosphere above these areas.

What If There Were No Sun?

Without the Sun, there would be no daylight. Without daylight, the sky would be black rather than blue. There would be no sunrises or sunsets, no clouds, and no weather.

 The aurora borealis is caused by solar wind particles crashing into particles in Earth's atmosphere above the Arctic.

The Sun Causes Earth's Seasons

Earth's four seasons are caused by the Sun. As it orbits the Sun, Earth is tilted at an angle. This means that different parts of Earth face the Sun at different times. From October to March the Southern Hemisphere faces the Sun, giving it longer and hotter days. From April to September, the Northern Hemisphere faces the Sun. That is why in December it is winter in North America and summer in Australia.

Years Are Measured by the Seasons

Years on Earth have always been measured by the seasons. For many cultures around the world, the beginning of one spring to the beginning of the next spring marks a year. This works out to be around 365 days.

What If There Were No Sun?

If there were no Sun, there would be no changes to temperature or weather at different times of the year. Earth would not have seasons.

Ⓥ The seasons are vital to life on Earth. They allow each part of the world to have a break from the harshness of the Sun's rays.

Sun Fact ☀

All life on Earth has adapted to the change of light and darkness over twenty-four hours. Night-time gives people, plants, and animals a chance to rest away from the strong light of the Sun.

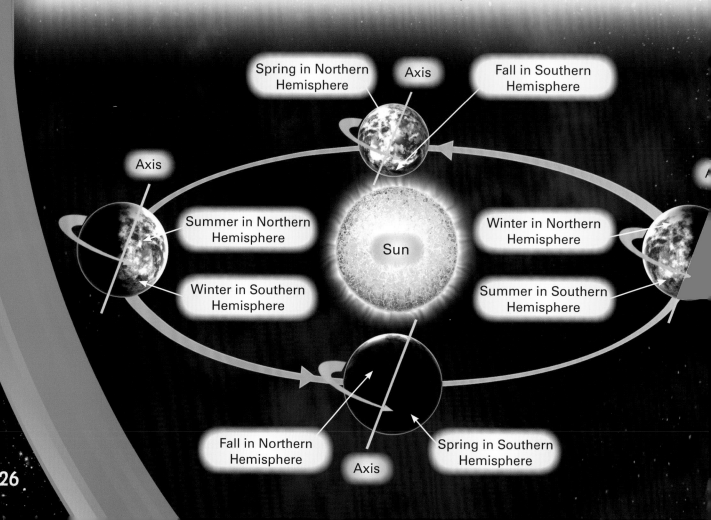

Spring in Northern Hemisphere

Axis

Fall in Southern Hemisphere

Axis

Summer in Northern Hemisphere

Winter in Southern Hemisphere

Sun

Winter in Northern Hemisphere

Summer in Southern Hemisphere

Fall in Northern Hemisphere

Axis

Spring in Southern Hemisphere

The Sun Helps Mark Earth's Time

Long before computers and calendars, people used the Sun to mark time. The movement of the Sun marked the passing of time during the day. It also marked years with the change of seasons.

Days Are Measured by the Sun

Days on Earth have always been measured by the Sun. It takes twenty-four hours for one place on the Earth to move from one midday to the next. This is because Earth is rotating on its axis, and it takes a day for it to completely turn around.

What If There Were No Sun?

Without a Sun, we would not have 24-hour days or 365-day years. There would be no way to mark regular time by daily and yearly rhythms.

FAMOUS SKY WATCHERS

It is believed that the Greek philosopher Oenopides was the first person to calculate Earth's tilt, in about 450 BCE. In the 1500s, astronomers Galileo Galilei and Johannes Kepler proved that Earth orbited the Sun. It was not until these two facts were put together that it was understood how Earth's tilt as it orbits the Sun creates the seasons.

Before clocks, sundials used shadows created by the Sun to show the time during the day.

WHAT DOES THE FUTURE HOLD FOR THE SUN?

Scientists think that the Sun will start to run out of fuel and die in about five billion years. But that will not be the end.

The Sun Will Become a Red Giant

In about five billion years, the Sun will run out of **hydrogen** and it will have to start using **helium** for energy. Helium will make the Sun grow bigger and burn brighter. The Sun will then become a red giant star. It could grow to be about 30 times larger than it is today. It will remain as a red giant for many millions of years.

Sun Fact

When the Sun becomes a red giant, it will grow so large that the four inner planets, including Earth, will be destroyed by its heat.

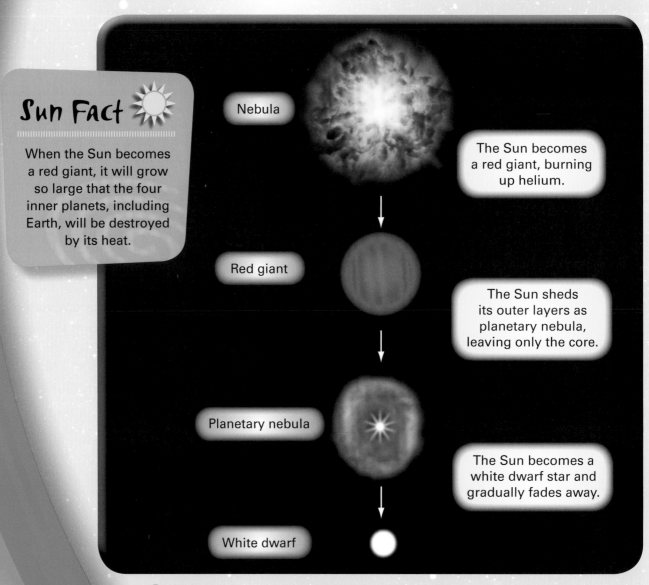

Nebula

The Sun becomes a red giant, burning up helium.

Red giant

The Sun sheds its outer layers as planetary nebula, leaving only the core.

Planetary nebula

The Sun becomes a white dwarf star and gradually fades away.

White dwarf

Over billions of years the Sun will become a red giant. Its core will then slowly cool and fade away.

The Sun Will Become a White Dwarf

When the Sun uses up its helium, its outer layers will fall away and only a small, white core will be left. The Sun will then be what is known as a white dwarf. It will slowly cool, fade, and crumble.

A New Star Will Be Born

When the Sun is finished, its dust and other space dust will form into new nebula. Over millions of years, gravity will start to pull the nebula together. It will then shrink and grow hot. From this nebula another star will be born.

V New stars are formed from the material left by old stars and solar systems. This nebula is called the Rosette Nebula.

FAMOUS SKY WATCHERS

In 1915, American astronomer Walter S. Adams identified the first white dwarf star. He named it Sirius B. From his observations, he worked out that although Sirius B is about the same size as Earth, it weighs as much as the Sun.

WHAT ARE THE SAFEST WAYS TO SUN-WATCH?

It is dangerous to look at the Sun directly. Instead, you can make a Sun projector. You will need an adult to help you make this and project the image.

1. Mark the shape of the binocular lenses on the card and cut a hole.
2. Prop up the second piece of cardboard to make a screen.
3. Facing away from the Sun, aim the binoculars at the Sun.

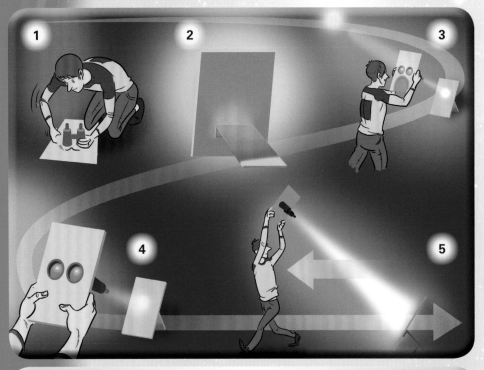

4. Turn the binoculars until the image of the Sun is projected clearly onto the propped-up cardboard.
5. To make the image larger, move farther away from the cardboard screen.

 Sun projection is the safest and easiest way to see the Sun without looking directly at it.

Use a Sun Projector

To look at the Sun indirectly, you can project its image onto paper or a screen.

You will need:

- binoculars (or a telescope of less than 4 in. (100 mm) and less than thirty magnification
- two pieces of white cardboard, about 16 x 16 in. (40 x 40 cm)
- a pencil and a pair of scissors.

Warning

You should not view the Sun directly, as it can harm your eyes. If you want to observe the Sun, use the Sun-projection method with the help of an adult. Otherwise, visit an observatory and ask for the help of an astronomer to observe the Sun.

Useful Websites

Explore the Sun: www.kidscosmos.org/kid-stuff/sun-facts.html

How the Sun Works: http://science.howstuffworks.com/sun4.htm

Sun: http://science.nationalgeographic.com/science/space/solar-system/sun-article.html

World Book at NASA: www.nasa.gov/worldbook/sun_worldbook.html

GLOSSARY

asteroids	Small, rocky, or metal space objects that orbit the Sun.
atmosphere	The layer of gases that surrounds a planet, moon, or star.
axis	An imaginary line through the middle of an object, from top to bottom.
comets	Small, rocky, and icy space objects that have long, shining tails that appear when orbiting near the Sun.
electric currents	The flow of electric energy, which can be carried by wire to produce heat and power.
equator	An imaginary line around the middle or widest part of a round space object, such as a star or planet.
galaxy	A large system of space objects, including stars, planets, gas, and dust.
gases	Substances that are not solid or liquid, and are usually invisible.
gravitational pull	The forces of gravity that attract two objects toward each other.
gravity	The force that attracts all objects toward each other.
helium	An air-like substance that is colorless and odorless; the second most common gas in the universe.
hydrogen	An air-like substance that is colorless, odorless, and can easily catch on fire; the most common gas in the universe.
magnetic currents	The flow of energy, produced by electrical charges, which can produce heat and power.
magnetic fields	Forces produced by electric currents.
meteoroids	Small space objects that are made of rock and metal, ranging from several feet wide to the size of a pea.
nebula	A cloud of gas and dust in space.
nuclear energy	Energy in the form of heat that is produced when two or more atoms (the smallest part of substance) join together to form a single new atom.
orbit	The path taken by a space object that travels around another, larger one.
particles	Very small parts of substances or matter.
plasma	An extremely hot gas that has become so hot it is sensitive to magnetism; found in the Sun and other stars.
protostar	A young star, in the form of a cloud of gas and dust, that has not yet started to create energy in its core.
radiation	Energy that travels in the form of waves or rays and can be harmful to living things.
rotates	Turns or spins around a fixed point or an axis, like a spinning top.
solar power	Energy that comes from capturing the heat of the Sun.
solar system	The Sun and everything that orbits it, including planets and other space objects.
space	The area in which the solar system, stars, and galaxies exist, also known as the universe.

INDEX